Lee Wade's
Korean Cookery

HOLLYM
Elizabeth NJ · Seoul

Lee Wade's Korean

Edited by Joan Rutt & Sandra Mattielli

HOLLYM

Cookery

Lee Wade's Korean Cookery

Copyright © 1985
by C.Ferris Miller
All rights reserved

Photographs Copyright© 1985
by Hollym Corporation; Publishers
All rights reserved

First published in 1974
by Pomso Publishers.

Second revised edition. 1986
Eleventh printing, 1999
by Hollym International Corp.
18 Donald Place, Elizabeth, NJ 07208, U.S.A.
Phone: (908)353-1655   Fax: (908)353-0255
http://www.hollym.com

Published simultaneously in Korea
by Hollym Corporation; Publishers
13-13 Kwanchol-dong, Chongno-gu, Seoul 110-111, Korea
Phone: (02)735-7551~4   Fax: (02)730-5149
http://www.hollym.co.kr

ISBN: 0-930878-45-0
Library of Congress Catalog Card No.: 85-80453

Printed in Korea

for
KIM SAMSUN
and
NO IMSUN

Contents

SWEET DISHES

Preface

Lee Wade was genuinely and deeply interested in cooking. Although at college she majored in history, her greater enthusiasm was for culinary affairs. As a schoolgirl she enjoyed helping to prepare food for large groups at summer camps; for the last ten years of her life, while she was working full time as a librarian with the Eighth US Army Recreation Services in Seoul and bringing up two small boys, she nevertheless found time to prepare several elaborate dinner parties at home every month, occasionally for as many as twenty guests at a time.

For these parties she drew on her collection of several hundred cookbooks to prepare dishes from different traditions of cuisine for the pleasure of guests of Korean, American and many other nationalities. In this she was helped by her long-time housekeeper Mrs Kim Samsun, to whom she had taught western cooking. Mrs Kim, in return, taught Lee Korean cookery. The original idea for this book came from that collaboration.

Sandra Mattielli and her cook, Mrs No Imsun, were brought into consultation, and Sandra did the spadework on the lists and illustrations of vegetables and fruits which were planned as part of the book.

Before the work had progressed beyond the stage of sheaves of notes and drawings, however, Lee was overtaken by the tragic illness from which she died on 20 January 1973 at the age of 36.

Her family gave her collection of multinational cookbooks to the Yongsan Army Library that she had so long served. The notes for her own Korean cookbook were entrusted to me for editing so that the book might be published as a memorial to Lee and a posthumous fruit of her interest in Korean food. Her many friends and acquaintances scattered all over the world will surely be glad to have this reminder of her delight in seeing others enjoy good cooking.

My work has been to check the recipes, test them in the kitchen and at the table, and rewrite some of them for publication. I have expanded the lists of vegetables, fruit and mushrooms, and added lists of fish and other foodstuffs in accordance with the plans outlined in the notes I received. Because of the personal nature of the collection, which it seemed particularly desirable to preserve, I have refrained from adding recipes that Lee had not either already prepared or left notes for. It remains Lee's book, not mine. Sandra Mattielli took up where she had left off in the collaboration before Lee fell ill. The design, illustrations, and book production are her work.

I received valuable suggestions from Mrs Pak Talsun of Pyŏng-ch'ŏn, in South Ch'ungch'ŏng, who went over the recipes with me in detail. Mrs Pak enjoys a well-earned reputation as a cook in an area of Korea that prides itself on the purity of its cultural tradition. My chief critic and helper from the point of view of practical gastronomy was my husband, Bishop Richard Rutt, who lived on Korean food for fifteen years, and was long looked after by a skillful cook who was trained as a bride in the traditions of the wealthier families from the north side of Seoul. He also did a great deal of dictionary work for this book, and obtained copies of invaluable Korean cookery-books for my reference. Many Korean friends, especially priests of the Anglican church, have helped with comments on the food I have prepared according to these recipes.

The most useful reference books were *Chosŏn yori chebŏp* by Pang Shinyŏng, first published in 1917 (there were 16 editions all told) and its successor *Uri nara ŭmshik mandŭnŭn pŏp* (1954). Miss Pang was the chief adviser for Harriet Morris's *The art of Korean cooking* (Tokyo and Rutland, Vermont, 1959) though Miss Morris deliberately adapted the recipes to suit American tastes. Another valuable book is Mrs Yun Sook's *Han-guk yori* (1973).

The usual standard for nomenclature, both Korean and scientific, of plants and animals, has been the dictionary *Kugŏ tae sajŏn,* edited by Yi Hŭisŭng (1961) and checked against the *Han-guk tongshingmul togam,* issued by the Ministry of Education. The six-volume edition of the Han-gŭl Society's dictionary *K'ŭn sajŏn* (1947-57) also contains useful information about Korean food—far more than one would expect from a dictionary.

A modern reference book that Lee and I both found useful is *Kajŏng yori paekkwa* by Pak Cheok ('Home cooking encyclopedia', 1965, reprinted 1972). *Chosŏn kungjŏng yori t'onggo* by Han Hŭisun, Hwang Hyesŏng and Yi Hyegyŏng, published in 1957, deals with the palace tradition, but I have used it for checking some details. The type of cooking in which Lee Wade was interested was not that of the palace tradition but middle-class home cookery, which is what this book represents. The seasonings have not been modified for western palates; they indicate what is popular today in central Korea.

The royalties from the sale of this book will be donated in memory of Lee Wade to the cancer research program of Chŏnju Presbyterian Medical Center.

Joan Rutt

How to Use This Book

This is a practical cook-book intended primarily for foreigners living in Korea who have had some experience of eating Korean food and want to try making it. It expresses the fascination of the infinite variety of Korean foods, especially vegetables and fish. These are not elaborate recipes, but good useful everyday food that can be prepared with a reasonable expenditure of labour and time. Special seasonal dishes like the *songp'yŏn* of the autumn moon festival have not been included; consequently this is nothing like a complete collection of Korean recipes. Those who want to make their own soy sauce, or pickle a supply of kimch'i for the winter, will need to consult Korean cook-books, some of the best of which are named in the preface.

Though this book contains a number of individual recipes that have not yet appeared in English, its chief original features are the descriptions of Korean *namul* (fresh vegetables and salads) with instructions for preparing and serving them, and the lists of foodstuffs with their names in *han-gŭl* and romanization as well as English. These lists are in *han-gŭl* alphabetical order, so that when you come across a new food name in Korean, you can look it up easily; if you need to find out the Korean name of any foodstuff, you can find that by using the general index.

ADAPTABILITY OF KOREAN RECIPES

The characteristic flavours of Korean food come from the methods of cooking and from the ingredients, not from using precise quantities of the main seasonings. This means that you should adapt the quantities, especially of things like salt, soy sauce, garlic, red pepper, sesame oil and onion, to suit your own and your family's taste. 'Individuality', Lee Wade wrote, 'is the key to Korean cooking.' A small quantity of chopped beef is regarded as a desirable condiment in many dishes, such as fish stews and fried squash; but beef is very expensive, and Korean cooks often omit the beef (e.g. in bean-sprout soup) where it is used only for flavour and is not a basic ingredient. Korean dishes can be as lavish or as frugal as you and your purse like.

So this book has been planned as a guide for foreigners who feel the urge to experiment and explore a new world of food.

MEASUREMENTS

Weights are given for things that have to be bought by weight. Metric equivalents for avoirdupois are given in approximations which are practical for market and kitchen. In Korea there is a steady movement in the direction of selling everything by metric weight, but it has still a good way to go.

Otherwise standard American cup and spoon measurements have been used (even for things like red pepper threads that are hard to persuade into tea-spoons) and all measures are level unless otherwise stated.

THE CLASSIFICATION OF THE RECIPES

A typical Korean meal consists of a bowl of rice and a bowl of soup for each person, and a number of other dishes which are usually shared. These side-dishes are called *panch'an,* and the more there are of them, the more elaborate the meal. Four is an average number for an everyday meal when there are no guests: there might be, for example, a meat or fish dish, one or two kinds of kimch'i, and a vegetable (*namul*) or bean curd. When there are guests a dozen or more *panch'an* may be served.

Sometimes, however, there is a dish which can constitute a meal by itself (e.g. *kimpap* or *mandu*), or which, when served with rice, does not require much if anything in the way of *panch'an* (e.g. *pulgogi*); these dishes are known as *yori.*

Sweet dishes have been given a section to themselves, though they are not usually served separately, but appear on the table along with the other *panch'an.* Fresh fruit, however, is often served at the end of a meal, peeled if necessary, and cut into suitable pieces.

NUMBER OF SERVINGS

It follows from what was said about the sharing of side-dishes (you usually help yourself with your chopsticks) that the concept of 'a serving' has little validity in the context of Korean meals; but generally speaking, the recipes in this book should be sufficient for four to six people.

MARKETING

It is easiest to begin shopping for Korean foods in one of the supermarkets, where you can help yourself to what you want and get an idea of the prices generally obtaining. The pleasure of shopping in a typical Korean market should on no account be missed, however. Foreign shoppers are generally very well looked-after by the traders, because they are regarded as guests. Your first expedition should preferably be when you do not need to buy much and have time to sightsee, for it is all a bit bewildering until you are used to the noise and the sheer array of goods.

The lists for identification of the various foodstuffs at the end of this book have not been overloaded by including western vegetables like celery or tomatoes, the names of which are the same as in English and which you can recognize when you see them. These lists do, however, include all the ingredients required for the recipes.

The lists (of fruits, seafood and cereals especially) do also include many items which are not mentioned in the recipes; this is in keeping with the aim of the whole book, which is to encourage western cooks to experiment with Korean food. Latin names have been given for fishes and plants, because their English names are not always familiar, and for the sake of readers who are interested in identifying the species.

Because most of the important foods have more than one name, the lists were difficult to compile, and doubtless still contain some errors, despite the care that has been taken. The wild sesame, for instance, is usually listed as *perilla frutescens,* but some books call it *perilla ocymoides.* The common Chinese cabbage has three Latin names (*brassica campestris, brassica pekinensis* and *brassica chinensis*) and six Korean: *paech'u, paech'a, paech'ae, pepch'u, paekch'ae* and *songch'ae.*

ONIONS

The many varieties of green onion have proved particularly difficult to identify. Green onions are very important in Korean cooking, and many different names for them can be heard in the markets as the seasons change. At different times of year the 'medium green onion' required in so many of the recipes is known by slightly different names, though they can all be called *p'a*. If the recipe calls for medium green onions, any green onion about 7″ to 12″ long with a white base may be used; and if 'thread onions' are specified, the kind to use are the fine-leaved varieties, 5″ to 10″ long and lacking a well-developed white base. Chives are a good substitute for thread onions.

SEASONAL AVAILABILITY

The last column in the lists of fruit, vegetables and seafood is no longer as important as it was even five years ago. A great many fruits and vegetables are produced out of season by means of PVC cloches and frames. Mushrooms, fish, seaweeds and some fruits are preserved by the traditional method of drying, and nowadays many kinds of fish are preserved by deep-freezing.

SUBSTITUTES

Anyone living in a western country who wishes to try these recipes should be able to find many of the necessary ingredients in oriental groceries in the cities. Imagination, supplemented by botanical knowledge, may suggest substitutes for some of the herbs and wild plants used.

In recipes requiring mushrooms, particular kinds have not been specified unless the character of the recipe depends on them. Many more kinds of fungi are commonly eaten in Korea than in America or Britain.

A FEW PRELIMINARIES

1. Preparing vegetables, etc.: Instructions have not been given about the careful washing and trimming of vegetables for use, or the gutting of fish and drawing and plucking of fowls which are often necessary. These are all taken for granted in the recipes that follow.
2. Cooking rice: Plain rice is prepared as follows: take ¾ cup of grain per person of average appetite, wash it twice, then rub it well with the hands to remove loose starch. Rinse it again. The grains must be rinsed once or twice more until the water runs clear. Inspect the clean rice and remove any foreign bodies such as small stones.

   Pour on to the rice, in the vessel in which it is to be cooked, 1 cup of cold water for every cup of rice used, or a very little more. A Korean cook estimates the water required, covering the rice to a depth of 1″, or enough to cover her hand spread flat on the surface of the rice. The grain may be allowed to soak in the water for an hour or so.

   Bring the rice and water quickly to boiling-point, reduce the heat and simmer for about 15 minutes until all the water is absorbed. If the bottom layer is toasted brown, *nurŭm-bap*, everybody likes it, especially the children. To serve, arrange the rice neatly in individual bowls. Rice is also prepared mixed with other grains, pulse, sweet potatoes or chestnuts.
3. Rice-water to drink: Water is boiled in the pan in which the rice was cooked,

and it takes flavour and sometimes colour from the rice that clings to the pan. (The pan is also easier to wash afterwards.) This water is served towards the end of the meal, or whenever people ask for water.

4. Barley tea: Put 4 tablespoonfuls of parched barley into a muslin bag and boil them for 1 to 1½ hours in 8 cups of water. This is often served before a meal. Ordinary barley can be parched on a griddle, but it is easier to buy barley ready parched.

5. Sesame salt is required in many savoury dishes; it is prepared by heating sesame seeds (ch'amkkae) gently in a strong pan until they turn brown and swell. They are then pulverized in a mortar with one teaspoonful of salt per cup of sesame seed.

6. Ginger and garlic for seasoning: These recipes say 'chop finely'; some recipes say 'crush'. But my Korean advisers say the flavour and texture are better for most recipes if these ingredients are chopped.

7. Eggs are prepared for decorating many dishes by frying the yolk and white separately in very thin sheets on a lightly-oiled pan. The sheets are then cut into diamonds or threads, according to the recipe for the dish you are decorating.

8. Vinegar and soy sauce, dip for fried foods: Mix soy sauce and vinegar in equal quantities; sugar may be added to taste. Pine nuts, sesame seeds and other additions are optional.

Abbreviations

lb(s) — pound(s)
oz(s) — ounce(s)
gr(s) — gram(s)
T — level tablespoonful
t — level teaspoonful

Romanization

In this book romanization of Korean words is according to the McCune-Reischauer system: the vowels are pronounced as in Italian and the consonants as in English.

Vegetables as Side-dishes

The Korean cuisine uses a wide variety of wild and cultivated plants as side-dishes and seasonings. Here are some of those which can be found in the markets, with a simple method of preparation for each. The lists do not claim to be exhaustive, but they provide a jumping-off point for enterprise in this fascinating branch of cookery.

Before preparation, the vegetables must be thoroughly washed and the wilted and spoiled parts removed. Many of them are so tender that if cooking is required it is enough to put them into a cup or so of boiling water ('scald'), cover and bring to a boil again, then drain immediately and douse with cold water ('refresh'); this helps to retain the original colour of the vegetable. If there is no safe supply of cold water, the vegetables may be scalded in salted water, without refreshing them afterwards; in this case the salt helps to retain the colour. Either way, the vegetables are drained and then mixed with a basic sauce, or the sauce may be used as a dip for them.

Basic Sauce
(for approximately one packed cup of washed vegetable)
Mix: 1 T soy sauce   1 t sugar
    ¼ t vinegar   1 T sesame salt
    ⅛ t sesame oil   a small pinch MSG, if liked

Some or all of the following may be added; see notes on the individual vegetables.

    1 t red pepper threads
    1 t red pepper paste
    1 young green onion or leek, finely chopped
    1 clove garlic, finely chopped
    1 t fresh ginger, finely chopped

The botanical names of the plants listed here will be found on pages 81-93.

ROOTS

Tŏdŏk The root of a mountain climber, available in the markets from March to May. A cultivated variety, less tasty, can be bought all through the winter at supermarkets.

Wash and scrape the roots, split them and beat each half flat with a mallet or kitchen knife-handle. Then soak them in water for about 10 minutes, squeeze dry, and dress with basic sauce + red pepper paste, leek and garlic.

Toraji Chinese bellflower root, available most of the year. It is best bought ready cut into slivers, and is then prepared like *muu saengch'ae* (see recipe, page 67).

Mulssuk namul This is a kind of mugwort, available from January to April. Boil it for 10 minutes, drain and mix with basic sauce + red pepper paste, onion, garlic and ginger.

Ingredients I

soy sauce (*kanjang*)

soy-bean paste (*toenjang*)

red pepper paste (*koch'ujang*)

salt (*sogŭm*)

sesame salt (*kkaesogŭm*)

sesame seed oil (*ch'amgirŭm*)

cooking oil (*shigyongyu*)

mustard (*kyŏja*)

B

Ingredients II

① white radish *(mu)*
② carrot (*tanggŭn*)
③ potato (*kamja*)
④ parsley (*p'asŭlli*)
⑤ lettuce *(sangch'u)*
⑥ onion (*yangp'a*)
⑦ green pepper (*p'utkoch'u*)
⑧ red pepper (*tahong koch'u*)

⑨ *minari*
⑩ bean sprout (*k'ongnamul*)
⑪ squash (*hobak*)
⑫ eggplant (*kaji*)
⑬ ginseng (*insam*)
⑭ dried persimmon (*kotkam*)
⑮ chestnut (*pam*)
⑯ jujubes (*taech'u*)

⑰ red pepper powder (*koch'u karu*)
⑱ pine mushroom (*songi pŏsŏt*)
⑲ ginger (*saenggang*)
⑳ garlic (*manŭl*)
㉑ egg (*kyeran*)

Ssŭmbagwi This is a member of the Milkweed family, available in March. The fresh root is very bitter. Barely cover it with water, boil until it is slightly softened and throw away the water. Cover it again with water, leave it to stand several hours and change the water. Do this several times during the day, and leave the root in a further change of water overnight. Next day, cut it into bite-sized pieces and mix with the basic sauce + red pepper paste, onion, garlic and ginger.

Yŏn-gŭn Lotus root, available all the year. Peel it like a potato, cut it into ¼"-thick discs (or ovals, by cutting diagonally, if you prefer; the section is very pretty), barely cover it with water and boil 15 to 20 minutes.

Pour off most of the remaining water, add 1 T soy sauce and 2 T sugar and simmer gently. Turn the slices over from time to time until they are all browned. Take off the heat and add 1 t sesame seed and ¹/₈ t sesame oil. Lotus root slices can also be candied.

Uŏng Burdock root, available all the year round. Peel it like a potato, cut it into diagonal slices, cover with water, boil for 20 minutes and drain. Add 1 t sesame seed and ¹/₈ t sesame oil, or cut it into shoestrings, deep fry, and sprinkle it with 1 t soy sauce, 1 T sugar and 1 T sesame seed.

GREENS

Ch'amjuk(sun) namul These are the tender shoots of the Chinese mahogany tree, *ch'amjuk namu* (from the wood of which farm tools and brides' trousseau-chests were traditionally made). They are only available for about two weeks in May, earlier in the south than in the north. Scald the shoots, refresh and drain. Mix with the basic sauce + onion, garlic and ginger.

Hoennip namul Tender shoots of the spindle, available for one week in April. Scald them, refresh and drain. Mix with the basic sauce without vinegar.

Kkaennip namul (*tŭlkkae*) Leaves of the wild sesame (*perilla frutescens* or *ocymoides*) sold in bundles in the markets in late summer and autumn. Scald, refresh and drain them, then mix them with the basic sauce + garlic and red pepper threads. The sesame oil may be increased to ¼ t or more, if liked. The leaves are served flat on a small shallow dish, and will keep some time in the sauce if refrigerated and closely covered.

Kosari Edible bracken, young shoots, gathered in April and May and sold fresh at that time, when they are delicious. Large quantities are also dried, and the *kosari* sold in the markets during the rest of the year have been soaked and boiled to swell them up again. Those that have been dried are not so good to eat as the fresh ones.

Wash the shoots carefully and cut off any damaged or stringy ends, then mix them with the basic sauce without vinegar, but with red pepper threads, and cook gently for 10 minutes. Or boil them in water for 10 minutes and then mix them with the sauce.

Kobi Osmunda fern; treat like *kosari*.

K'ongnamul Bean sprouts (of the yellow soy bean), available all the year round. Can be grown at home, if desired. After washing the sprouts and breaking off the hairlike root, put them wet into a pan and steam them for 10 minutes over gentle heat. Mix them with basic sauce, without vinegar but with onion, garlic and red pepper. Bean sprouts are also used in many recipes.

Sukchu namul or *noktu namul* Sprouts of the green or mung bean, available all the year. Prepare them like *k'ongnamul.*

Minari This aromatic plant, important in Korean cookery, has no exact western equivalent, though parsley can be substituted for it in some recipes. Its botanical name is *oenanthe stolonifera,* and it belongs to the same family as the evening primrose. It grows in water, and therefore should be very carefully washed and preferably scalded before use.

It appears in the markets as bunches of thin stems 6" to 12" long, with dissected leaves at one end of the bunch. It is usually the stems, cut into 1" or 2" lengths, that are called for in Korean recipes, but the leaves can be included when minari is prepared for the table as *namul* (salad). The leaves also add a delicious smoky fragrance to soup, and are good with fish.

To prepare *minari namul,* scald it, refresh and drain. Mix with the basic sauce + red pepper threads. Serve cut into lengths, or tied.

Naengi Shepherd's purse, available in March and April. The familiar weed, gathered from waste ground and baulks between fields, is sold in flat bundles in the market. The whole plant is collected, complete with its long white tap-root. To prepare *naengi* for cooking, remove dead leaves and wash the plants well, then cut off the tap-root just below the rosette. Boil for 10 minutes; dress with basic sauce + onion, garlic and red pepper threads.

Sangch'u Lettuce, sold as leaves, not heads. (Head lettuce is sometimes available in markets that cater for foreigners.) Wash the leaves thoroughly, put a drop of sesame oil in the last washing water, and arrange the leaves to look like a large flower on the dish. Serve the basic sauce plus onion in a small dish, to dip the leaves in.

Shigŭmch'i Spinach, available in spring, autumn and winter; the Korean variety is smaller than western leaf spinach, though the taste is the same. The whole plant is usually uprooted and sold. Typically it consists of a flattish rosette of dark green leaves attached to the short stem and a small part of the root. Wash the plants, removing the root and any spoiled leaves; very large plants may be cut in halves or quarters, so that the pieces when cooked are a suitable size to take with chopsticks and eat at a mouthful. Keep the leaves attached to a piece of stem.

Scald the prepared plants in boiling water, turning them over once while bringing the water back to boiling point. Do not over-cook. Save the water for soup. Refresh and drain, then mix the spinach with the basic sauce minus vinegar, + onion, garlic and red pepper threads.

Ssukkat The garland chrysanthemum, also known as chop suey greens, available most of the year (not usually in the hottest part of summer). Scald the shoots, refresh, drain, and dress with the basic sauce without vinegar, + onion, garlic and red pepper threads. *Ssukkat* is also served uncooked, with red pepper sauce, or the basic sauce as a dip. If you grow it yourself you will probably like to serve it raw.

Turŭp namul Shoots of the angelica tree (opening buds), available in April and May. They are sold in long straw plaits. The buds should be boiled for a few minutes, refreshed and drained; serve them dressed with the basic sauce, or serve the sauce separately as a dip.

Wŏnch'uri Young shoots of a day-lily, *hemerocallis aurantiaca,* available in spring. They are tied into small knots, scalded and drained, then mixed with the basic sauce.

ONIONS AND OTHER BULBOUS PLANTS

There is a great variety of onions and similar species, and some confusion over their names. A list with botanical names, as far as they can be identified, will be found on page 83. Most of them are chiefly used as seasoning, but the following appear on the table as side-dishes in their own right:

Manŭl Garlic is served pickled (see recipe, page 66) and also in its natural state: the cloves are peeled and cut into thin flat slices. This makes a very powerful side-dish, eaten in small quantities with other food. Green garlic, *p'unmanŭl,* available March-May, is eaten cut into 2 " lengths and dipped in red pepper paste. In May, when the flower-heads of the plant appear, the long green flower-stems, *manŭlchong,* are sold in bunches. These are cut into 2 " or 3 " lengths and either eaten raw or boiled for a few minutes. Either way, they are served with the basic sauce + 1 T red pepper paste.

Pibich'u This is really a variety of hosta, not an onion. It is available in March. Scald, refresh and drain them, then mix with the basic sauce + red pepper paste.

Puch'u A kind of wild leek, available most of the year. Scald, refresh, drain and cut them into 2 " lengths, then mix them with the basic sauce + red pepper threads.

Tallae A wild onion, available in spring and autumn. Scald them, refresh and drain. The leaves are wrapped round the neck of the bulb. They are served with the basic sauce + red pepper threads.

Tangp'a A green onion that grows in clusters, available in spring and autumn. Their chief use is as seasoning, but very young ones can be served like *tallae.*

Green Onion Soup *Tangp'aguk*

¼ lb (100 grs) beef, cut into
   thin 1″ squares
4 T soy sauce
2 cloves garlic, finely chopped
½ T sesame salt

black pepper to taste
5 cups water
5 medium green onions
1 beaten egg

1. Put the beef in a pan with the soy sauce, garlic, sesame salt and black pepper, and cook over good heat till the meat is seared and brown, not red, in colour.
2. Add the water and cook for 30 minutes or until the meat is tender.
3. Cut the green onions into 1″ lengths and mix them with the egg.
4. Pour the mixture a little at a time into the boiling soup and cook gently for 5 minutes.
5. Check the seasoning and serve.

21

Seaweed Soup *Miyŏkkuk*

½ lb (225 grs) brown seaweed (miyŏk)
¼ lb (100 grs) lean beef, thinly sliced
3 cloves garlic, finely chopped
1 t sesame salt
3 T soy sauce
2 t sesame oil
½ t black pepper
½ t MSG

1. Wash and soak the seaweed in water for 1 hour; then drain it and cut into 2″ pieces.
2. Put the beef in a pan with the garlic, sesame salt, soy sauce, sesame oil and pepper, and cook until the meat is brown.
3. Add the seaweed and 6 cups water, and simmer for 30 minutes, or until the seaweed is tender.
4. Add MSG, check seasoning, bring back to the boil and serve.

Bean-sprout Soup *K'ongnamulkuk*

¼ lb (100grs) beef
3 T soy sauce
1 t sesame oil
3 cups prepared bean
  sprouts
2 t sesame salt
6 medium green onions or
  a handful of chives
2 beaten eggs
black pepper to taste

1. Thinly slice the beef and cook in the soy sauce and sesame oil till it changes colour.
2. Add 1 cup water and the bean sprouts, and simmer until tender.
3. Add 6 cups water and the sesame salt; boil for 10 minutes.
4. Cut the onions or chives into 1″ lengths and mix them with the eggs. Drizzle this mixture into the soup.
5. Check the seasoning, adding pepper to taste, and serve immediately.

Bean-sprout soup is often made without meat or eggs; in this case add 3 cloves of finely-chopped garlic to the soy sauce and sesame oil at the beginning, and sprinkle in ½ t MSG (if liked) just before adding the green onions.

Rib Soup *Kalbit'ang*

2 lbs (900 grs) short ribs of beef
10 cups water
5 T soy sauce
6 large green onions or leeks, sliced in rings
  (including the green part)
1 head garlic, finely chopped
2 T sesame salt
½ t black pepper
salt to taste, if needed
1 egg, prepared for decoration

1. Have the ribs cut into pieces 2″ long; score the meat thoroughly.
2. Cook the ribs in 10 cups of water until the meat is tender; this may take up to 2 hours. The water should boil gently, not much above simmering point.
3. Take the ribs out of the liquid and cook them with the soy sauce, onion, garlic, sesame and pepper until these seasonings are well absorbed (about 5 minutes).

4. Skim excess fat off the liquid in which the ribs were boiled, and put the ribs with seasonings back into it. Simmer for ½ an hour.
5. Check seasoning and serve, decorating each bowl of soup with egg strips.

Chicken Soup *Takkogiguk*

1 small whole chicken
6 cups water
3 potatoes, diced
1 carrot, diced
1 T soy sauce
1 large green onion or leek, chopped
3 cloves garlic, finely chopped
¼ t black pepper

1. Cook the chicken in the water for one hour.
2. Add the remaining ingredients and cook for a further ½ hour.
3. Take out the chicken and remove the flesh from the bones, putting the flesh back into the soup in pieces of a suitable size for eating with a soup-spoon.
4. Check the seasoning, reheat, and serve.

Soy-bean Paste Soup *Toenjangkuk*

6 cups water
4 T soy-bean paste (toenjang)
1 packed cup shepherd's purse (naengi) prepared by washing thoroughly and then cutting the leafy part from the tap-root. Both leaves and root are used.
½ cup outside leaves of Chinese cabbage, shredded
2 leeks, cut in fine rings
2 cloves garlic, finely cut
¼ t MSG

1. Bring the water to a hard boil with the soy-bean paste.
2. Add the shepherd's purse and the Chinese cabbage. Cook rather fast for 30 minutes.
3. Stir in the leeks and garlic, bring back to the boil and simmer for 3 minutes.
4. Sprinkle in the MSG and serve.

27

Dumpling Soup   *Mandukuk*

3 cups mung bean sprouts
1 young squash (summer only)
1 lb ground beef (450 grs)
2 cakes bean curd (300 grs each)
1 green pepper, finely chopped
1 head garlic, finely chopped
2 T sesame salt
2 t sesame oil
3 T soy sauce
2 leeks, chopped
2 carrots, chopped
¼ cup chopped mushrooms (p'yogo, if available)
salt and black pepper to taste
3 cups flour
1 cup water

1. Remove the bean as well as the hairlike tip of each bean sprout; cook the sprouts in boiling water for a short time until tender. Drain them and chop.
2. Cut the squash into thin slivers, sprinkle them with salt, and allow them to stand five minutes. If squash is out of season, 1 cup of lightly-boiled, chopped Chinese cabbage may be used instead.
3. Put the bean sprouts, cabbage or squash, beef and bean curd in cheesecloth and squeeze tightly to remove moisture. Then mix them with the green pepper, garlic, sesame salt, sesame oil, soy sauce, leeks, carrots and mushrooms. Finally add black pepper to

taste, and salt if necessary, mix well, check and adjust the flavouring.

4. Make a dough with the flour and water, kneading well. Shape the dough into a long sausage 1″ in diameter, cut it into 1″ lengths and roll out each piece into a 3″ circle on a floured board.

5. Put one tablespoonful of the meat mixture in the middle of each circle, fold over and crimp the edges well together.

6. Drop the mandu into boiling beef broth or green onion soup. When they rise to the surface, cook for 2 minutes more. Serve at once, in the bowls of soup. About six mandu per person is right for a first helping, but if they are being served without side-dishes you may need a dozen or more per person.

Beef Ball Soup *Wanjaguk*

½ lb (225 grs) ground beef
1 cake bean curd
1 T soy sauce
2 medium green onions, finely chopped
2 cloves garlic, finely chopped
1 T sesame salt
¼ t black pepper
1 t sesame oil
2 T pine nuts
1 beaten egg
flour
1 recipe Green Onion Soup (see page 21)

1. Mix the beef, bean curd, soy sauce, onion, garlic, sesame salt and oil, and black pepper thoroughly together.
2. Take the mixture by level teaspoonfuls and roll into balls; press 2 pine nuts into each ball.
3. Roll the balls in beaten egg and then in flour, and fry till brown in a lightly-greased pan.
4. Add the balls to the green onion soup, bring to the boil and simmer very gently for a few minutes, check seasoning and serve.

Picnic Rice in Seaweed *Kimpap*

1. Cook the rice in the water. It should not be moist after cooking.
2. Cut the beef into thin strips and fry it with the soy sauce, onion and sesame oil.
3. Cut the pickled radish and carrot into thin strips.
4. Fry the beaten egg yolks and whites separately in thin layers and cut them into thin strips.
5. To assemble, cover a sheet of laver with a thin layer of rice, leaving a strip one inch wide uncovered along the edge furthest away from you. Two inches in from the near edge and parallel to it, lay the strips of beef, radish, carrot, egg white and yolk, pieces of spinach and red pepper threads. Beginning with the near edge, roll it up as you would a jelly-roll (Swiss roll). The vegetables and meat will be in the centre. Seal the roll by moistening the uncovered further edge of the laver and pressing the roll down on it.
6. Fill the other sheets of laver in similar fashion.
7. With a sharp knife dipped in cold water, cut the rolls into 1″ slices to serve or pack into lunch-boxes.

2 cups rice
2¼ cups cold water
½ lb (225 grs) lean beef
2 T soy sauce
1 dry onion, finely chopped
1 t sesame oil
1 yellow pickled radish
1 undercooked carrot
4 eggs, separated
½ cup cooked spinach
1 t red pepper threads
20 full-sized sheets of laver

Skewered Mushrooms *Songi Sanjŏk*

8 fresh songi mushrooms
1 lb (450 grs) lean beef
8 T soy sauce
4 t sugar
2 T chopped medium green onion
4 cloves garlic, finely chopped
2 t sesame salt
½ t black pepper

1. Cook the mushrooms by boiling them in water.
2. Slice them lengthwise in strips ⅛" thick, and slice the beef into pieces the same size.
3. Marinate both beef and mushrooms in the remaining ingredients for 2 hours.
4. Thread pieces of beef and mushrooms alternately on skewers and broil them.

Skewered Beef and Onion *P'a Sanjŏk*

1½ lb (650 grs) beef, not too lean
the green tops of 6 large leeks
4 T soy sauce
1 T sugar
1 T chopped green onion
2 cloves garlic, finely chopped
2 T sesame salt
¼ t black pepper
1 T sesame oil
2 T rice wine

1. Cut the beef into ½"×3" strips. Cut the onion tops into 3" lengths.
2. Marinate the beef in the remaining ingredients for 2 hours.
3. Skewer the meat slices alternately with the onion tops.
4. Brush the marinade on the meat and onion tops while broiling them.

Mung Bean Pancake *Pindaettŏk*

4 cups dried mung beans, prepared by
   crushing, to split the skins
salt to taste
water

1. Soak the beans in water overnight, for
   ten or twelve hours.
2. Cover the beans with fresh water and
   rub between the hands to remove the
   skins, which will float to the top of the
   water. Repeat this process until all the
   skins are removed; drain well.

3. Grind the beans in a mortar or blender.
   Add enough water to make a thick
   paste. Season with a little salt; do not
   make the batter too salty as the finished
   product is usually dipped in soy sauce
   at the table.
4. Drop the batter by tablespoonfuls on to
   a heated greased pan or griddle and
   cook like pancakes, browning lightly on
   both sides.

This is the basic recipe, but it is usual to

34

Mung bean pancake mixed with meat and vegetables.

add many kinds of shredded vegetables, especially minari, to the batter before frying. Pork or beef, shredded and fried beforehand, is also sometimes added. The quantities depend on what is available and on whether this is a main dish or one among a number of *panch'an;* suitable quantities for the above volume of batter if a fairly substantial main dish is required are:

    1 lb (450 grs) shredded pork, fried in a small amount of oil till well done
½ cup minari stems, cut in 1″ lengths and scalded
2 leeks, chopped
1 head garlic, finely chopped
1 T sesame salt
1 t fresh ginger root, fineiy chopped
½ cup paech'u kimch'i, chopped

Any or all of these ingredients should be well mixed with the bean batter before it is fried.

Beef and Mushrooms   *Soegogi Pŏsŏt Pokkŭm*

1 lb (450 grs) tender beef, cut in thin slices
10 large mushrooms, cleaned and sliced
3 T soy sauce
4 small green onions, cut into 1″ lengths
3 cloves garlic, finely chopped
½ t fresh ginger, finely chopped
1 T sesame salt
¼ t black pepper
2 T sesame oil
½ cup water

1. Fry all the ingredients together until the beef and mushrooms are cooked.
2. The water can be added a little after the frying begins, and a smaller quantity may be sufficient, depending on how much liquid the mushrooms produce. If necessary, the liquid can be thickened before serving with 1 T cornstarch mixed in 1 T cold water.

Broiled Beef *Pulgogi*

1 lb (450 grs) beef, not too lean (fat and lean streaked is best)	4 medium green onions, coarsely chopped
2 T soy sauce	3 cloves garlic, finely chopped
1 T sugar	1 t fresh ginger, finely chopped
1 T sesame oil	
1 T sesame salt	2 T water, rice wine or
$^1/_8$ t black pepper	white wine

1. Cut the beef into thin slices about 3″ square by $^1/_8$″ thick. This can be done at the butcher's shop.
2. Marinate the beef in the remaining ingredients for up to 1½ hours.
3. Traditionally, this meat is broiled at the table on a Korean pulgogi grill over charcoal, gas ring or hotplate. Otherwise, use a frying-pan or oven-broiler.

Pork is also cooked in this way, or a combination of meats can be used.

Fried Fish with Vegetables *Saengsŏn Yach'aejŏn*

A 1 lb (about 450 grs) croaker (minŏ) or
  other firm fish
  20 medium shrimps
  1 t salt
  1 T finely-chopped green onion
  3 cloves garlic, finely chopped
  1 T fresh ginger, finely chopped
  ¼ t black pepper
  1 t sesame oil
  1 T rice wine
B 15 medium green peppers

  ½ t salt
  ½ t sesame oil
C ½ a medium carrot
  ¼ t salt
  ½ t sesame oil
D 10 p'yogo mushrooms, fresh or dried
  ¼ t salt
  ½ t sesame oil
E ½ cup flour
  3 eggs

1. Finely chop the croaker and shrimp meat and mix them together; season with the remaining A ingredients and mix again. Shape into neat rectangles.
2. Seed the peppers, cut into thin strips and sprinkle with the salt. After 10 minutes, wash, drain and mix the pepper strips with ½ t sesame oil.
3. Cut the carrot into thin strips, salt for 10 minutes, wash, drain and mix with ½ t sesame oil.
4. If dried mushrooms are used, soak them in lukewarm water for 15 minutes. Then cut the mushrooms, whether fresh or dried, into thin strips and season them with salt and sesame oil.
5. Dip the fish rectangles first into flour and then into beaten eggs. Arrange strips of pepper, carrot and mushroom on top of each rectangle. Dip again in flour and then in beaten egg.
6. Fry in a lightly-greased pan until brown.

Noodles with Meat and Vegetables *Chapch'ae*

A ½ lb (225 grs) lean beef
   ¼ lb (100 grs) pork
   3 T soy sauce
   1 T sugar
   1 T sesame salt
   ½ t black pepper
   2 T sesame oil
B ⅓ lb (150 grs) Chinese noodles
   (tangmyŏn)
   1 cup cooked spinach

C 2 large carrots cut into matchsticks
   10 medium green onions cut into 1″
   lengths
   5 wild leeks (puch'u)
   2 dry onions, chopped
D 3 p'yogo mushrooms
   10 mogi mushrooms
   5 nŭt'ari mushrooms
   10 sŏgi mushrooms

1. Cut the beef and pork into fine strips and fry with the other A ingredients until well cooked and tender.
2. Cook the noodles in plenty of boiling water until soft; rinse in cold water.
3. Fry the C ingredients gently together in a lightly-greased pan for 10 minutes to soften, not brown.
4. Soak the p'yogo, mogi and nŭt'ari mushrooms in warm water for 10 minutes, then cut them into strips and fry in the same way as you fried the vegetables.
5. Immerse the sogi mushrooms in boiling water for 2 minutes, then cut them into strips.
6. Combine all the ingredients including the spinach; heat before serving, or the dish may be served cold.

This dish is sometimes made with a larger proportion of noodles.

Rib Stew   *Kalbitchim*

2 lbs (900 grs) short ribs of beef, sawn into
  2″ lengths
2 T sugar
2 T sesame oil
½ cup soy sauce
3 medium green onions, chopped
1 head garlic, finely chopped
3 T sesame salt

1 carrot
6 mushrooms, sliced
1½ cups water
2 T rice wine
2 T pine or ginkgo nuts
1 egg for decoration (see page 14)
¼ t black pepper
1 T flour

1. Score each piece of meat deeply with a sharp knife several times, and marinate them with the sugar and sesame oil for 1 hour.
2. Add the soy sauce, onions, garlic, sesame salt, pepper and flour to the meat and mix well.
3. Cut the carrot diagonally into oval slices ¼″ thick, and add them to the meat with the mushrooms and water.
4. Cook for about one hour, rather gently. When the meat is tender, add the rice wine and bring the stew back to the boil.
5. Sprinkle ginkgo or pine nuts on top before serving and decorate with strips of egg.

43

Stuffed Squid *Ojingŏ Sundae*

2 fresh squids (large)
½ carrot
2 dried mushrooms
10 ginkgo nuts
2 cakes of bean curd
1 cup cooked noodles
¼ t minced ginger
¼ t MSG
½ t sugar
½ t salt
1 T soy sauce
1 cup fish stock

1. Remove the tentacles from the squids and chop the tentacles finely.
2. Skin the bodies of the squids and clean them.
3. Mince the carrot, mushrooms and nuts; mix these with the bean curd, noodles, ginger, and seasonings, and with the chopped tentacles, and loosely stuff the fishes with the mixture. Skewer the opening.
4. Steam for ½ an hour, then boil in the stock for 5 minutes.
5. To serve, cut each fish crosswise into slices ½″ thick.

44

Fried Croaker *Minŏjŏn*

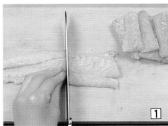

1 lb filleted croaker
½ t salt
¼ cup flour
2 T oil (butter is better, if available)

2 T soy sauce
¼ t black pepper
1 cup small green onions, cut in halves
1 cup green peppers cut in slivers

1. Cut the fish in pieces 1″×4″, dip them in seasoned flour and fry them in the oil or butter till browned on both sides.
2. Add the following ingredients on top:
   1 t red pepper threads

3. Cook gently for 2 minutes, then turn over carefully and cook gently for 2 minutes more. The onions and peppers should be arranged attractively on top in the serving-dish.

Fried Dried Anchovies   *Myŏlch'i Pokkŭm*

2 cups dried anchovies
¼ cup cooking oil
¼ cup soy sauce
1 T sugar
2 T sesame salt
MSG, if liked

1. Wash the anchovies and drain well.
2. Mix them with oil and fry for three minutes.
3. Add the remaining ingredients and cook for 2 more minutes.
4. These are eaten in small quantities, as one of a number of side-dishes.

Dried squid (ojingŏ) may be prepared in exactly the same way after it has been cut into thread-like strips.

Fried Oysters   *Kuljŏn*

1 lb (450 grs) oysters
flour
3 eggs slightly beaten
salt and black pepper

1. Wash the oysters and pick them over carefully, as they often have pieces of shell mixed with them.
2. Drain them well, dip them first in flour and then into beaten egg, and fry in a lightly-greased pan.
3. Season them to taste with salt and pepper, and serve hot.

Clam Meat in the Shell *Taehaptchim*

10 large clams
¼ lb (100 grs) ground beef
1 T soy sauce
½ t vinegar
1 medium green onion, chopped
1 clove garlic, finely chopped
½ t sesame salt
⅛ t red pepper powder
⅛ t black pepper, freshly ground
⅛ t MSG

1 cake bean curd, mashed

1. Remove the clams from the shells, wash them, drain and chop them fine.
2. Mix the beef, soy, vinegar, onion, garlic, sesame salt, peppers and MSG.
3. Combine the chopped clams beef mixture and mashed bean curd, and fill the 20 half-shells with the mixture.
4. Steam the filled shells for 40 minutes.

Crisp Laver *Kim Kui*

10 sheets laver
1 T sesame oil
1 T salt

1. Examine the sheets of laver and brush off any sand.
2. Spread the sheets one at a time on a board, brush with sesame oil and then sprinkle lightly with salt.
3. Put the sheets on a grill, griddle or skillet over low heat and cook a few seconds till crisp.
4. Cut each sheet into four or six pieces, and serve piled on small plates. These are so light that they blow about, and are sometimes anchored by sticking a toothpick vertically through the layers.

They are usually eaten wrapped around rice, but some people like them as they are.

Salted Beef   *Changjorim*

¼ lb (100 grs) lean beef
2 cups boiling water
⅓ cup soy sauce
3 T sugar
1 t fresh ginger root,
    chopped

The meat should be in one or two pieces cut with the fibres running from end to end, about 3″ long. Meat shops in Korea supply suitable pieces if you say you want meat for changjorim.

1. Cook the beef in the water until it is tender. Drain off the water to use for soup.
2. Add the soy sauce, sugar and ginger to the beef in a small pan, cover and simmer very gently till little liquid remains. Be careful that the meat does not burn.
3. Tear the meat into small strips to serve it.

Liver with Onions *Kan Pokkŭm*

½ lb (225 grs) liver
¼ t salt
1 T fresh ginger root, finely chopped
2 medium-sized dry onions, chopped
1 T soy sauce
1 T sugar
1 T sesame salt
¼ t sesame oil
black pepper to taste

1. Cut the liver into bite-sized pieces, sprinkle it with the salt and ginger, and let it stand for 30 minutes, turning it over occasionally.
2. Brown the liver in a lightly-oiled pan.
3. Add the onion and cook gently for 10 minutes, to soften, not brown, the onion.
4. Add the remaining ingredients and ⅓ cup water. Cook for five minutes.
5. If it is too thick, add a little more water; if too thin, thicken with a little cornstarch mixed with cold water.
6. Check the seasoning and serve hot.

Fried Cucumbers *Oi Pokkŭm*

6 cucumbers
1 T salt
¼ lb (100 grs) lean
   ground beef
A 2 t soy sauce
  1 medium green onion,
   chopped
  1 T sesame salt
  ¼ t black pepper
  1 T sesame oil
B 2 T soy sauce

1 T sugar
2 medium green onions,
  chopped
1 t fresh ginger, finely
  chopped
2 cloves garlic, finely
  chopped
½ t red pepper powder
½ t MSG
C 1 T sesame seed
  ½ t red pepper threads

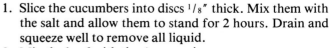

1. Slice the cucumbers into discs ⅛″ thick. Mix them with the salt and allow them to stand for 2 hours. Drain and squeeze well to remove all liquid.
2. Mix the beef with the A seasonings.
3. Put the beef mixture and the cucumbers in a pan and sprinkle with the B seasonings. Fry until the beef is cooked.
4. Serve hot or cold with the sesame seed and red pepper threads (C) arranged on top as a decoration.

Dried Squash   *Hobak Pokkŭm*

1 cup dried squash
2 T soy sauce
1 T sugar
1 medium green onion, chopped
2 cloves garlic, finely chopped
1 T sesame salt
½ t red pepper powder
1 t sesame oil

1. Soak the squash in warm water for 10 minutes.
2. Cut it into fine strips and mix with the remaining ingredients.
3. Cook for 10 minutes over low heat.
4. Serve hot or cold.

Stuffed Green Peppers *Koch'ujŏn*

15 large green peppers
½ lb (225 grs) beef
1 T soy sauce
1 medium green onion,
  chopped
2 cloves garlic,
  finely chopped
½ t sesame salt
¼ t black pepper
⅛ t MSG
1 t sesame oil
flour
2 beaten eggs

1. Cut the peppers in half lengthwise and remove the seeds.
2. Mince the beef and mix it with the soy sauce, onion, garlic, sesame salt, black pepper, MSG and sesame oil.
3. Stuff the pepper halves with the beef mixture, and put the two halves of each pepper together again.
4. Dip the peppers into flour and then into beaten egg.
5. Fry until golden in a lightly-oiled pan.
6. Serve hot or cold.

Fried Mushrooms   *Pŏsŏtchŏn*

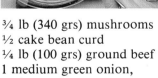

¾ lb (340 grs) mushrooms
½ cake bean curd
¼ lb (100 grs) ground beef
1 medium green onion, chopped
1 clove garlic, finely chopped
½ t sesame salt
½ t sesame oil
1 t sugar
salt
black pepper
flour
2 eggs

1. Wash the mushrooms and remove the stems, keeping these for soup.
2. Mash the bean curd, squeezing out the liquid. Mix the curd with the beef, onion, garlic, sesame salt and oil, sugar, salt and pepper to taste.
3. Sprinkle the insides of the mushroom caps with flour, then fill them with the meat mixture.
4. Dip the filled mushrooms first in flour, then in beaten egg, and fry in shallow fat, or grill.

Fried Squash   *Hobakchŏn*

1 young squash, the long
  shape, not the round
½ T salt
2 ozs (50 grs) lean beef
½ T soy sauce
1 t vinegar
1 t sesame salt
1 t sesame oil
1 clove garlic, finely
  chopped
2 T flour
1 egg, beaten
1 T oil for frying

1. Slice the squash into discs ¼″ thick, sprinkle with salt and allow them to stand 10 minutes. Drain off the liquid and dry the discs with cloth or kitchen paper.
2. Mince the beef and mix it with the soy sauce, vinegar, sesame salt and oil, and garlic.
3. Spread each disc of squash with the beef mixture, then dip it first in flour and then in beaten egg.
4. Fry gently until the squash is cooked.
5. Serve with a mixture of equal quantities of soy sauce and vinegar. The food is dipped into this mixture just before being eaten.

56

Eggplant in Soy Sauce   *Kajitchim*

4 medium eggplants
salt
2 ozs (50 grs) lean beef
3 T soy sauce
1 green onion, finely
  chopped
1 clove garlic, finely
  chopped
1 t sesame salt
1 t sesame oil
½ t vinegar
1½ T sugar
2 green onions, cut in 1″
  lengths
1 T water

1. Cut each eggplant across into 3 pieces; slit each piece twice through the centre without cutting through the ends (as you cut a cucumber for kimch'i, see page 64).
2. Sprinkle them with salt and leave for 15 minutes, then drain.
3. Mince the beef and season it with 1 t soy sauce, onion, garlic, sesame salt and oil.
4. Stuff the eggplant pieces with the beef mixture, then put them in a pan and sprinkle with vinegar, sugar, green onions, water, and the remaining soy sauce.
5. Bring to the boil and simmer gently until the liquid is almost all evaporated.

Steamed Eggs   *Altchim*

3 eggs
A 1 t soy sauce
   1 T water
   1 young green onion,
     chopped
   ½ t sesame salt

⅛ t red pepper powder
⅛ t black pepper powder
¼ t salt
B ½ a young green onion,
     chopped
   ⅛ t red pepper threads

1. Beat the eggs. Add the ingredients in list A and mix well.
2. Pour the mixture into a small greased pan or casserole and sprinkle the ingredients in list B over the top.
3. Steam for 10 minutes and serve immediately. This mixture must not boil.

Vegetable Omelet   *Puch'imgae*

1. Prepare the bean sprouts by removing the hair-like root of each.
2. Cook the bean sprouts, green onion and puch'u in a lightly oiled pan until they are tender, sprinkling them lightly with salt to taste.
3. Squeeze the squash pieces in a cloth to remove the moisture, and cook them in a lightly-oiled pan.
4. When the vegetables are cool, stir them into the beaten eggs.
5. Spoon about one-fifth of the mixture into a heated oiled pan, distribute the vegetables evenly, and fry the omelet over medium heat till it is golden brown on both sides. Repeat until the mixture is used up; it should make 5 omelets, 6″ in diameter.

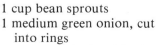

1 cup bean sprouts
1 medium green onion, cut into rings
½ cup puch'u (or chives) cut in 4″ lengths
1 young squash, cut into 2″-long matchsticks and salted
2 T scalded minari, chopped
6 eggs, lightly beaten with a sprinkle of salt
oil   salt

Fried Bean Curd   *Tubu Puch'im*

1 cake bean curd
3 T cooking oil
3 T soy sauce
5 small green onions (thread onions or chives) cut in 1″ lengths
1 t red pepper threads
¹/₈ t black pepper
2 T sesame salt

1. Cut the bean curd into slices ¼″ or ⅓″ thick. Fry them in the oil over low heat till light brown on both sides.
2. Sprinkle with the rest of the ingredients and cook 2 minutes more on each side.

Red Pepper Paste Stew   *Koch'ujang Tchigae*

4 cups water from the third washing of rice
4 T red paper paste
1 cake bean curd, cut in 1" squares, ¼"
  thick
20 small green thread onions, cut in halves
½ head of garlic, finely chopped
1 cup bean sprouts, prepared by removing
  the hairlike tips (the roots)
½ cup bellflower root (toraji), shredded
¼ t MSG

1. Mix all the ingredients, cover, and boil
   5 minutes. Simmer for 10 minutes
   more, check seasoning and serve piping
   hot.

This stew is often enriched with a little
finely-chopped beef, and fish, especially
salted fish, is very commonly added to it.
Salted fish should be soaked beforehand,
cut to suitable size, and added with all the
other ingredients. Fresh fish should not be
added till after the 5 minutes' boiling of
the other ingredients.

Chinese Cabbage Kimch'i *Paech'u Kimch'i*

2 Chinese cabbages
1¼ cup salt
1 medium white radish
½ cup red pepper powder
⅓ cup salted baby shrimp
2 t fresh ginger, finely chopped
1 head garlic, finely chopped
1 cup minari stems, cut in 1″ pieces
¼ cup small green thread onions or chives, cut in 1″ lengths
¼ cup very thin green onion, cut in 1″ lengths
⅓ lb fresh oyster
red pepper thread

1. Cut each cabbage in half lengthwise.
2. Make a brine with 10 cups water and 1 cup salt and soak the cabbage sections in the brine.
3. When the cabbages are well-salted, rinse thoroughly in cold water and drain.
4. Cut one-third of the radish into thin strips.
5. Mix the red pepper powder well with the salted shrimp juice. Add the mixture to the radish strips and mix well until the reddish color is set. Then add the remaining ingredients. Season with salt.
6. Pack the seasoned mixture between each leaf of the wilted cabbage. Cut the remaining radish into large pieces and mix it with the seasoned mixture.
7. Place the stuffed cabbages and radish pieces in a large crock.

Hot Radish Kimch'i *Kkaktugi*

This recipe is for a smaller quantity with fewer ingredients, for use through the year.

2 medium white radishes, cut into 1″ cubes
3 T red pepper powder
3 T salt
½ head garlic, finely chopped
2 t fresh ginger, finely chopped
¼ cup small green thread onions or chives, cut in 1″ lengths
1 t sugar
¼ t (a good pinch) MSG
1 T red pepper threads

1. Rub the cut-up radish well with the red pepper powder (wear gloves), and allow it to stand for 30 minutes.
2. Mix in first 2½ T salt, then the remaining ingredients.
3. Put the mixture into a suitable jar, sprinkle with the remaining ½ T salt, cover the kimch'i and put a weight on top. It will make enough liquid; you do not usually need to add water to this kimch'i.

It will be ready to eat after 2 days at room temperature, or after 24 hours in hot weather, but will keep for up to a week (more in cold seasons) if stored, closely covered, in a refrigerator.

Cucumber Kimch'i *Oi Sobagi Kimch'i*

10 fresh young cucumbers, thin ones
5 green onions, finely chopped
1 head garlic, finely chopped
2 T fresh ginger root, finely chopped
red pepper threads or powder
3 T salt
2 t sugar

1. Cut the cucumbers into 4″ lengths. Slit each piece twice through the middle, with the two cuts at right angles and without cutting through the ends. Rub them with salt (extra to the 3 T above) and let them stand for an hour to soften.

2. Mix the onion, garlic, ginger, red pepper, salt and sugar. The quantity of red pepper depends on your taste, and thread pepper is less hot than powder. About 1½ or 2 T will probably be enough .

3. Taste the filling before adding the last tablespoonful of salt; you may find that 2 or 2½ T are enough.

4. Rinse the cucumbers lightly and fill the cuts with the mixture. Be careful not to put too much of the mixture into the first cucumber pieces; it may help to divide the filling and the cucumber pieces into four equal parts before you begin.

5. Pack the pieces into a jar and just cover with brine. About 30 hours is enough for fermentation in summertime.

6. To serve, cut each 4″ piece of cucumber into 2 pieces through the middle, and serve them cut side up in a shallow dish, so that the stuffing shows.

White Radish Kimch'i *Nabak Kimch'i*

2 medium white radishes (about 700 grs each)

⅓ cup of green onion, cut in 1"-long thin strips

1 cup minari stems, cut in 1" pieces and scalded

½ a head of garlic, finely chopped

1 t fresh ginger root, finely chopped

1 T red pepper threads

2 T salt

10 cups water

1. Cut the radishes into rectangles about ¾" × ¾" and ⅛" thick. Sprinkle them with the salt, and turn the mixture over to make sure the salt comes in contact with all the radish pieces. Allow to stand for an hour.

2. Mix all the remaining ingredients except the water. The quantities of these ingredients are variable according to your taste, and you should experiment to find out what suits you best. Some people add sugar or MSG, etc, but these are not in the classic recipes.

3. Drain the liquid from the radish squares, saving it. Mix the radish squares with the spices and vegetable mixture, put it all in a kimch'i jar and add the salt water that you drained from the radishes, diluting it to make 10 cups of brine. Taste this, and add more salt if necessary.

Allow the kimch'i to ferment for 2 days at 70°F. It will take longer in cooler weather and less time in very hot weather. Kimch'i is ripe when the liquid no longer tastes like brine. It will keep in a refrigerator for several days after ripening, but the jar must be very closely covered.

Pickled Garlic   *Manŭl Changatchi*

1 quart whole young garlic (i.e., 4 cups, but measure it in a larger vessel, as you will get more heads of garlic into it)
1 cup vinegar
4 cups soy sauce
⅔ cup sugar

1. Prepare the garlic by taking off any dry skin from the outside. Do not separate the heads into cloves.
2. Put the garlic in a jar, add the vinegar and enough water to cover the garlic. Make sure the garlic is covered and does not float. Close the jar and allow to stand one week. Drain.
3. Boil the soy sauce with the sugar for 10 minutes, and allow it to cool. Pour it over the garlic, and seal the jar.
4. The garlic is ready to eat after three weeks, but it will keep indefinitely.
5. To serve it, slice across into discs 1/8″ thick.

Garlic suitable for preserving in this way can be bought in April or May in Korea. It needs to be so young that the inner membranes surrounding the individual cloves are really tender, so that you can eat the whole thing.

66

Hot Shredded Radish *Mu Saengch'ae*

1 large white radish,
  weighing about 3 lbs
1 T salt
3 T red pepper powder
10 small green thread
  onions or chives, cut in
  1″ lengths

2 cloves garlic, finely
  chopped
1 T vinegar
1 T soy sauce
1 T sesame seeds
¼ t MSG, if liked
1 T salt

1. Cut the radish into slivers, sprinkle with 1 T salt and
   allow it to stand for 5 minutes. Rinse and drain well,
   then squeeze it dry.
2. Mix the radish first with the red pepper powder, then
   with the rest of the ingredients. Add the soy sauce
   before the salt, and check the saltiness before adding
   the full tablespoonful of salt.

If you like it less hot, use less red pepper, say 4 t, and
add a little sugar.

Lettuce Bundles *Sangch'ussam*

leaf lettuce
cooked rice
A 1 medium green onion, chopped
   2 T red pepper paste
   1 T soy bean paste
   1 T sesame seed
   ½ t sesame oil

1. Wash the lettuce well. Add a drop of sesame oil to the last water.
2. Mix the A ingredients to make a sauce, to be served in a small dish.

   At table, take a lettuce leaf, put on it a spoonful of rice and a little sauce, roll up the leaf and eat the bundle.

Black Soy Beans   *K'ongjaban*

1 cup black soy beans
1 cup cold water
¼ cup sugar
½ cup soy sauce
1 T sesame oil
1 t sesame seed
½ t red pepper threads

1. Wash the beans, put them in the water and boil them for 15 minutes.
2. Add the sugar, soy sauce and sesame oil, and continue to cook over low heat for 10 minutes. Just before the beans are ready add the sesame seed and red pepper threads.

Board with Nine Sections *Kujŏlp'an*

This dish is rather like *hors d'oeuvres,* in that it usually precedes the main meal and accompanies drinks. Special trays are made for it, consisting of a central compartment for the crêpes and eight surrounding compartments for the accompaniments. These are arranged so that their colours and textures contrast pleasantly.

To eat kujŏlp'an, put a little of each of the accompaniments on to a crêpe, add a little of the sauce, fold up and eat.

The eight accompaniments:

A ½ lb (225 grs)   ½ t sugar
    lean beef   1 clove garlic,
   1 t soy sauce   finely chopped
   1 T chopped   1 t sesame salt
    dry onion   ½ t sesame oil

1. Slice the beef into fine strips and season it with the other ingredients. Fry it in a greased pan until tender and allow it to cool.

B 2 large cucumbers   ½ t pine-nut flour
   1 t salt   black pepper
   ½ t sesame salt   ½ t sesame oil

2. Peel the cucumbers and slice them into fine strips. Mix with the salt. After 10 minutes, wash them in cold water and drain well. Fry the cucumber strips in a lightly-greased pan for 2 minutes, then mix them with the remaining B ingredients and allow them to cool.

C 10 sŏgi mushrooms   ½ t pine-nut flour
   1 t soy sauce   black pepper
   ½ t sesame salt   ½ t sesame oil
   1 t chopped dry onion

3. If the sŏgi mushrooms are dried, soak them, then immerse in boiling water and wash thoroughly until the water runs clear. Cut them into fine strips and fry them with the soy sauce and onion. Cool them, and season them with the remaining ingredients.

D 10 p'yogo mushrooms and the same

70

seasoning ingredients as C.

4. Deal with the p'yogo mushrooms in exactly the same way as the sŏgi mushrooms.

E 2 abalone   1 t sesame seeds
    1 t chopped dry onion   1 t sesame oil
    1 t soy sauce

5. Boil the abalone for 5 minutes. Remove the shells and black part. Slice the white part into fine strips and fry with the onion. Cool it and season with the remaining ingredients.

F 3 medium carrots   2 t sesame salt
    2 t soy sauce   2 t sesame oil
    2 t chopped dry onion

6. Cut the carrots into fine strips, fry them with the remaining ingredients, and allow to cool.

G and H
    5 eggs, separated

7. Fry the yolks and whites separately in very thin layers on a lightly-greased pan. Cut both into fine strips 2″ long.

Crêpes:
    1 cup flour   ½ t salt
    1½ cups water

8. Mix the flour, water and salt, and beat until the batter is smooth. Drop by spoonfuls on to a hot frying pan to make very thin crêpes 4″ or 5″ across, the exact size depending on the size of the central compartment of your dish with nine divisions into which they must fit.

Sauce:
    2 T water   1 t sugar
    2 T mustard   ½ t salt
    ½ t vinegar

9. Mix these ingredients.

This dish has many variants—tripe, minari, spinach, bean sprouts, squash, pork are all possible alternative 'accompaniments', so you can choose according to the season and the taste of your family. There are also two main styles for this dish, court and country.

71

Sweet Spiced Rice   *Yakshik*

4 cups glutinous rice
2 cups chestnuts
20 dried jujubes
¼ cup sesame oil
½ cup dark brown sugar
¼ cup pine nuts
2 T soy sauce
½ t powdered cinnamon
1 cup flour

1. Wash the rice, cover it with warm water and allow it to stand for 2 hours.
2. Drain, and steam the rice for 30 minutes.
3. Boil the chestnuts for 10 minutes, and peel them.
4. Soak the jujubes in warm water for 30 minutes, and pit them.
5. Mix the rice, chestnuts, jujubes, sesame oil, brown sugar, pine nuts, soy sauce and cinnamon. Make sure the fruit and nuts are well distributed.
6. Pack the mixture firmly in a bowl.
7. Add enough water to the flour to make a thick paste, and completely cover the rice mixture with this paste. Aluminium foil can be used instead of this paste.
8. Put the bowl into a pan containing boiling water enough to come halfway up the side of the bowl, and steam for 5 hours, adding more water as it boils away.
9. Lift the edge of the dough or foil to check the colour of the rice underneath. The dessert is done when the rice has turned dark brown. If it does not turn dark enough for your taste, you can add (Korean cooks often do) caramel to the mixture before putting it in the bowl to steam it.
10. To serve, remove the dough or foil and cut the dessert into cubes or rectangular pieces.

Jujube Balls *Choran* / Chestnut Balls *Yullan*

(Jujube Balls)

(Chestnut Balls)

(Jujube Balls)
1 oz dried jujubes (28 grs),
   about 15 jujubes
2 T honey
½ t cinnamon
3 T pine nuts

1. Soak the jujubes for 30
   minutes, and steam
   them for half an hour.
2. Pit the jujubes and
   chop them finely, then
   mix with the honey and
   cinnamon.
3. Shape into small balls,
   about ½″ in diameter.
   Roll them in chopped
   pine nuts.

(Chestnut Balls)
5 cups chestnuts
4 T honey
1 t cinnamon (powdered)

1. Cook the chestnuts in
   their shells till they are
   tender. Skin and mash
   them.
2. Mix the chestnut purée
   with the honey and cinnamon.
3. Shape the mixture into
   small balls and roll
   them in chopped pine
   nuts.

Dried Persimmon Slices / Skewered Ginkgo Nuts
Kotkamssam / *Unhaeng Kkoch'i*

(Dried Persimmon Slices)

(Dried Persimmon Slices)

10 medium dried persimmons
30 peeled walnuts

1. Remove the bases from the persimmons, take out the seeds and fill the cavities with walnuts.
2. Cut the persimmons crosswise into ½"-thick slices.

(Skewered Ginkgo Nuts)

1 cup shelled ginkgo nuts
¼ cup sugar
½ t sesame oil

1. Fry the nuts in a lightly-greased pan, and while they are hot, remove the skins.
2. Mix the sugar with the sesame oil and cook the nuts in the mixture.
3. Skewer five or six nuts on small sticks to serve.

Stuffed Jujubes   *Taech'uch'o*

30 dried red jujubes
10 chestnuts
⅓ cup water
⅓ cup honey
powdered cinnamon
3 T chopped pine nuts

1. Steam the jujubes for 6 minutes, and pit them.
2. Boil the chestnuts for 10 minutes, peel them and mash the kernels.
3. Fill the jujubes with mashed chestnut.
4. Simmer the stuffed jujubes in water and honey for 8 minutes, stirring constantly, but very gently.
5. Remove the jujubes, sprinkle them with cinnamon, and roll them in chopped pine nuts.

75

Candied Ginseng *Insam Chonggwa*

10 medium roots of fresh ginseng cut into
¼″ lengths
3 cups sugar

1. Cover the ginseng roots with water and
   simmer them for 30 minutes until they
   are well cooked.
2. Drain off the water and add the sugar
   to the ginseng. Cook very slowly over
   the lowest possible heat until no syrup
   remains and the ginseng is sticky.

Fried Honey-cakes   *Yakkwa*

2 cups flour
¼ cup sesame oil
2 T honey
2 T sugar
3 T rice wine
oil for frying
2 cups honey
½ t powdered cinnamon
½ cup finely-chopped fresh
   citron or 1 T finely-
   chopped ginger
½ cup finely-chopped pine
   nuts

1. Mix the flour, sesame oil, honey, sugar and wine, and knead the dough till it is smooth.
2. Roll the dough to ¼″ thick, and cut with a round cutter 1½″ in diameter.
3. Prick each circle of dough with a fork.
4. Heat the frying-oil to 300°F and deep-fry the cakes until they are light brown and float to the surface. Take them out of the oil then and drain.
5. Mix the 2 cups of honey with the cinnamon and citron. Soak the hot cakes in this mixture for 30 minutes, then remove and roll them in pine nuts.

77

Thin Cookies   *Maejagwa*

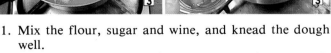
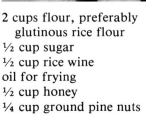

2 cups flour, preferably
   glutinous rice flour
½ cup sugar
½ cup rice wine
oil for frying
½ cup honey
¼ cup ground pine nuts

1. Mix the flour, sugar and wine, and knead the dough well.
2. Roll it out ⅛″ thick, and cut into rectangles 1″ × 1¾″. Cut three slits in each piece and twist one end through the middle slit.
3. Deep-fry in oil at 350°F until they are light brown; take them out and while they are still hot, dip them into the honey and then into the pine nuts.

These can also be made as flat cakes, kangjŏng, either round or square. For parties, they are often tinted.

Fruit Punch *Hwach'ae*

1 cup sliced fresh fruit
1 cup sugar
4 cups water
2 T pine nuts
powdered cinnamon

1. Mix ¼ cup of the sugar with the fruit and allow it to stand 30 minutes.
2. Boil the remaining ¾ cup of sugar with the water for 5 minutes, and allow to cool.
3. Mix the fruit and syrup and serve ice-cold, with pine nuts and cinnamon sprinkled on top.

Honey can be used, if available, instead of sugar; the perfume is more delicate, but the quantities may need adjusting.

Persimmon Punch   *Sujŏnggwa*

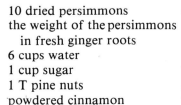

1. Scrape the ginger and slice it thinly. Add the water, and simmer for 1½ hours.
2. Remove the ginger and add the sugar to the liquid, boil for 5 minutes and cool.
3. Carefully remove the seeds from the persimmons and replace them with pine nuts. Add the persimmons to the syrup, and allow it to stand for 5 hours.
4. Chill the punch and serve it in a bowl with pine nuts and cinnamon sprinkled on top.

10 dried persimmons
the weight of the persimmons
   in fresh ginger roots
6 cups water
1 cup sugar
1 T pine nuts
powdered cinnamon

The quantities may be doubled, or the sugar increased to 1½ cups if a sweeter syrup is liked. Alternatively, the sugar may be replaced with honey. One of the pleasures of this dish is its delicate perfume.

Lists for Identifying Korean Foodstuffs

VEGETABLES AND HERBS

HAN-GŬL	ROMANIZATION	COMMON ENGLISH NAME	BOTANICAL NAME	AVAILABLE
갓	kat	Indian mustard *haruna* (Japanese)	brassica juncea	spring, autumn
가지	kaji	eggplant, aubergine	solanum melongena esc.	summer, autumn
깻잎	kkaennip	sesame leaves	perilla frutescens	summer, autumn
고비	kobi	osmund fern	osmunda japonica	(fresh) spring (dried) all year
고사리	kosari	bracken, young shoots	pteridium aquilinum	(fresh) spring (dried) all year
근대	kŭndae	chard	beta vulgaris	spring, autumn
냉이	naengi	shepherd's purse	capsella bursa-pastoris	Feb-April
녹두나물	noktu namul	mung bean sprouts	phaseolus radiatus	all year
돌나물	tol namul	stonecrop, deer's tail	sedum sarmentosum	March-May
두릅나물	turŭp namul	angelica tree, young shoots	aralia elata	April-May
미나리	minari	minari	oenanthe stolonifera	spring, summer, autumn
배추	paech'u	Chinese cabbage	brassica chinensis	most of the year
비비추	pibich'u	hosta, young shoots	hosta longipes	March
산쑥	sanssuk	mountain mugwort	artemisia gigantea	spring
상추	sangch'u	lettuce leaves	lactuca scariola	spring, autumn
쑥	ssuk	mugwort	artemisia asiatica	spring

쑥갓	ssukkat	garland chrysanthemum, shun-giku (Japanese), 'chop-suey greens'	chrysanthemum coronarium	spring to autumn
숙주나물	sukchu namul	mung bean sprouts	phaseolus radiatus	all year
시금치	shigŭmch'i	spinach	spinacia oleracea	autumn to early summer
아욱	auk	marsh mallow	malva verticillata	spring, autumn
오이	oi (oe)	cucumber	cucumis sativus	spring, summer, autumn
원추리	wŏnch'uri	day lily, young shoots	hemerocallis aurantiaca	spring
죽순	chuksun	bamboo shoots	phyllostachys edulis	April/May
참죽	ch'amjuk namul (ch'amjuksun namul)	young shoots of Chinese mahogany	cedrela sinensis	2 weeks in May
참취	ch'amch'wi	young leaves of a kind of aster	aster scaber	spring
콩나물	k'ongnamul	soy bean sprouts	glycine max (soya)	all year
팥	p'at	red bean	phaseolus angularis	all year (dried)
풋고추	p'utkoch'u	unripe chilli (green pepper)	capsicum annuum	summer, autumn
호박	hobak	squash, pumpkin, vegetable marrow	cucurbita moschata	summer, autumn
애호박	ae-hobak	a young squash		
긴호박	kin-hobak	a long squash, not round		
횟잎나물	hoennip namul	young shoots of the spindle	euonymus alatus	one week in April

ROOTS

감자	kamja	potato	solanum tuberosum	most of the year

고구마	koguma	sweet potato	ipomea batatas	most of the year
당근	tanggŭn	carrot	daucus carota sativa	most of the year
더덕	tŏdŏk	tŏdŏk	codonopsis lanceolata	spring, summer
도라지	toraji	bellflower root	platycodon glaucum	all year
마	ma	yam	dioscorea batatas	autumn, winter
물쑥	mulssuk	mugwort	artemisia selengensis	January-April
무	mu	giant white radish	raphanus sativus	all year
단무지	tanmuji	(pickled, yellow)	var. acanthiformis	
씀바귀	ssŭmbagwi	a kind of milkweed	ixeris dentata	March
연근	yŏn-gŭn	lotus root	nelumbo nucifera macrorhizimata	spring, autumn
우엉	uŏng	burdock root	arctium edule	all year
인삼	insam	ginseng	panax schinseng	all year
토란	t'oran	taro	colocasia antiquorum	autumn, winter

ONIONS AND GARLIC

달래	tallae	small wild onion	allium monanthum	spring
당파	tangp'a	medium green onion	allium fistulosum	spring, autumn
마늘	manŭl	garlic (ripe, dry)	allium sativum	all year
부추	puch'u	a small wild leek	allium odorum	most of the year
실파	shilp'a	'thread onion', like chives, but stronger		spring, summer, autumn
양파	yangp'a	'Spanish' onion (dry)	allium cepa	all year
움파	ump'a	winter scallion,		
황파	hwangp'a	cellar-grown (yellow)	? allium fistulosum	winter

83

청파	ch'ŏngp'a	medium green onion for spring use; these are grown in autumn, covered through the winter and marketed in early spring	? allium fistulosum	early spring
풋마늘	p'unmanŭl	green garlic	allium sativum	March-May
호파	hop'a	leek	allium porrum	autumn, winter

FRUITS

감	kam	persimmon	diosporos kaki	autumn
땡감	ttaeng kam	hard persimmon		
연시	yŏnshi	soft sweet persimmon		
곳감	kotkam	dried persimmon		all year
고욤	koyom	wild persimmon	diosporos lotus	early winter
귤	kyul	orange, 4 kinds:		
광귤	kwang kyul	sour yellow orange ('Seville')	citrus aurantium	winter
여름귤	yŏrŭm kyul	pomelo (rough skin, bitter)	citrus natsudaidai	summer
귤	kyul	dessert orange, many varieties, some imported	citrus nobilis	autumn (those from Cheju-do) all year (imported)
온주귤	onju kyul	Satsuma, small dessert orange	citrus unshu	November-December
딸기	ttalgi	strawberry	fragaria chiloensis	May and June
대추	taech'u	jujube, Korean date dried jujube	ziziphus jujuba	autumn all year

매실	maeshil	Japanese apricot	prunus mume (provides the 'plum blossom' of poets)	June / all year, salted
모과	mogwa	Chinese quince, used for medicine	chaenomeles sinensis	autumn
무화과	muhwagwa	fig	ficus carica	summer, autumn
배	pae	pear	pyrus sinensis / pyrus simonii	autumn, winter, spring

This is the roundish, crisp Chinese pear; the western kind are uncommon, but can sometimes be bought.

복숭아	poksunga	peach	prunus persica	June-September

There are many varieties, white, yellow and red-fleshed, freestone and clingstone. The yellow varieties are slightly more acid than the white. When buying peaches, feel or taste one, for they are too often picked long before they are ripe. NB the following names:

수밀도	sumildo: a name for various kinds of sweet and juicy peaches, originating in China (lit: 'water-honey-peach')
천도	ch'ŏndo: a smooth-skinned peach with acid-sweet flavour ('heavenly peach')

비파	pip'a	loquat	eriobotrya japonica	summer
사과	sagwa	apple	malus pumila	most of the year

The five best kinds of apple grown in Korea are:

국광	kukkwang	'national glory'	deep red with green, striped	best after Christmas
골덴딜리셔스	kolden dillisyŏsŭ	'golden delicious'	clear yellow, sweet, well-flavoured	best before Christmas
후지(부사)	huji (pusa)	'fuji'	light red	best about Christmas
인도	indo	'India'	green	best about Christmas
홍옥	hongok	'red jade'	bright red	best in autumn

There are no cooking apples, as there is no tradition of cooking fruit, but there is a crab-apple though it is now very rare:

능금	nŭnggŭm	Korean crab-apple	malus asiatica	autumn
살구	salgu	apricot	prunus ansu	2 weeks in June
수박	subak	watermelon	citrullus vulgaris	summer
석류	sŏngnyu	pomegranate	punica granatum	autumn
오얏	oyat	see *chadu*		
유자	yuja	citron	citros junos	winter (cf *kyul*)
자두	chadu	plum (several kinds)	prunus saliana typica	late summer
참외	ch'amoe	muskmelon, two varieties:smooth and yellow, or green and rough	cucumis melo	summer
포도	p'odo	grape (several kinds)	vitis vinifera	late summer, autumn

Buy grapes late in the season, in September; most Korean grapes are picked too soon.

NUTS

개암	kaeam	hazel	corylus heterophylla	autumn
밤	pam	chestnut	castanea crenata	(fresh) autumn (dried) all year
실백	shilbaek	see *chat*, pine nut		
은행	ŭnhaeng	ginkgo nut	ginkgo biloba	autumn (dried) all year
잣	chat	pine nut	pinus koraiensis	all year
호도	hodo	walnut	juglans sinense	(fresh) October (dried) all year

FUNGI

Most of these are available fresh in summer and autumn, and the important kinds can be bought dried throughout the year. The botanical names seem not to be clearly established, and where the reference books differ or give two names, both are listed below.

갓 버 섯	kat pŏsŏt	parasol mushroom	lepioptera procera	see note above
노루궁둥이	noru kungdungi	'roe-deer's rump'	hydnum erinaceus	
느 타 리	nŭt'ari (nŭt'arae)	an edible agaric	agaricus subfunereus, pleurotus ostreatus	
들싸리버섯	tŭlssari pŏsŏt	field mushroom	psalliota campestris	
목 이	mogi	Jew's-ear	auricularia polytricha, auricularia auricula-judae	
석 이	sŏgi	stone mushroom	gyrophora esculenta	
송 이	songi	pine mushroom	tricholoma matsutake, armillaria edodes	
싸 리	ssari	clavaria, twiggy mushroom	clavaria botrytis	
표 고	p'yogo	Japanese *shiitake*	lentinus edodes, cortnellus shiitake	

FISHES

Fish, fresh and dried, is plentiful and excellent in Korea. Most of the important coarse fishes are available out of season dried, frozen or salted. The last column suggests when the fish is at its best.

가 자 미	kajami	sole	limanda yokohamae	December
갈 치	kalch'i	cutlass-fish	trichiurus lepturus	August-October
게	ke	crabs	(numerous species)	June-July
고 등 어	kodŭngŏ	mackerel	scomber japonicus	February-September

꽁지	kkongch'i	mackerel pike	cololabis saira	May-Christmas
광어	kwangŏ	see nŏpch'i		
굴	kul	oysters	several species of ostrea	
낙지	nakchi	octopus	octopus vulgaris	summer, autumn
넙지	nŏpch'i	Korean halibut	paralichthys koreanicus	February-June
농어	nongŏ	Japanese sea-bass	lateolabrax japonicus	
대구	taegu	cod	gadus macrocephalus	winter
대합	taehap	clams	meretrix meretrix lusoria	early summer
도루무(묵)	torumuk (-mok)	sand-fish	arctoscopus japonicus	summer
도미	tomi	porgy (5 of the varieties):	sparidae (family)	summer
감성돔	kamsŏngdom		mylio macrocephalus	
붉돔	puktom	red porgy	boynnis japonica	
참돔	ch'amdom	true porgy (the best)	chrysophrys major	
청돔	ch'ŏngdom	blue porgy	sparus aries	
황돔	hwangdom	yellow porgy	taius tumifrons	
동태	tongt'ae	pollack	theragra chalcogramma	winter
멸치	myŏlch'i	anchovy (most important dried)	engraulis japonica	
명태	myŏngt'ae	pollack	theragra chalcogramma	
문어	munŏ	octopus	octopus vulgaris	summer, autumn
미꾸라지	mikkuraji	a kind of loach	misgurmus anguillocaudatus	
민어	minŏ	croaker	nibea imbricata	summer

방 어	pangŏ	horse-mackerel	seriola quinqueradiata	
뱀 장 어	paemjangŏ	eel	anguilla japonica	
뺑 어	paengŏ	ice-fish	salangichthys microdon	
뼈 오 징 어	ppyŏ-ojingŏ	cuttle-fish	sepia esculenta	
평 어	pyŏngŏ	butterfish	pampus argenteus	summer, autumn
복 어	pogŏ	globe-fishes (several species)	tetraodontoidei	spring
북 어	pugŏ	dried pollack	theragra chalcogramma	all year
붕 어	pungŏ	crucian carp	carassius auratus	early summer
삼 치	samch'i	a kind of bonito	sawara niphonia, cybium niphonia	early summer
새 우	saeu	shrimps (several species)	macroura	spring
서 대 기	sŏdaegi	tongue-fish	rhinoplagusia japonica	autumn, winter
숭 어	sungŏ	grey mullet	mugil cephalus	midsummer
연 어	yŏnŏ	Pacific salmon	onchorhynchus keta	autumn, winter
오 징 어	ojingŏ	squid (very important dried)	doryteuthis bleekeri	summer all year
은 어	ŭnŏ	sweetfish	plecoglossus altinelis	autumn
임 연 수 어	imyŏnsuŏ	sculpin	pleurogrammus azonus	winter
잉 어	ingŏ	carp	cyprinus carpio	spring, early summer
장 어	changŏ	octopus	octopus vulgaris	
정 어 리	chŏngŏri	sardine	sardinops melanosticta	autumn
전 복	chŏnbok	abalone	halliotis gigantea	
조 기	chogi	corvenia	pseudo-sciaena (a general name for a number of species)	April-July

HAN-GŬL	ROMANIZATION	ENGLISH NAME		NOTES
춘저	chunch'i	shad	ilisha elongata	summer
청어	ch'ŏngŏ	herring	clupea pallasii	winter
해삼	haesam	sea cucumber	stichopus japonicus	

SEAWEEDS

These are available most of the year, either dried or fresh.

김	kim	laver	porphyra tenera
녹미채	nongmich'ae	spindle-shaped bladderleaf	cystophyllum fusiforme
다시마	tashima	sea-tangle, kelp	ulva pertusa
해태	haet'ae		
모자반	mojaban	gulfweed	sargassum fulvellum enerve
미역	miyŏk	brown seaweed	undaria pinnatifida
청각	ch'ŏnggak	sponge seaweed	codium fragile
파래	p'arae	green laver	ulva conglobata

HAN-GŬL	ROMANIZATION	ENGLISH NAME	NOTES

CEREALS AND PULSE

가루	karu	flour, powder	as in *mil karu*, wheat flour; *kyep'i karu*, powdered cinnamon, etc
기장	kijang	panicled millet	also called broomcorn millet
녹두	noktu	mung beans	used for sprouts and bean curd
녹말	nongmal	mung bean starch powder	for thickening, etc
당면	tangmyŏn	Chinese noodles	made of potato flour
두부	tubu	(soy) bean curd	used in many dishes

Korean	Romanization	English	Description
메귀리	megwiri	oats	rarely if ever used as human food
메밀	memil	buckwheat	curd, noodles
묵	muk	curd (like jelly)	made from acorns, buckwheat, mung beans
밀	mil	wheat	eaten boiled with rice
뺑미	paengmi	polished rice	
보리	pori	barley	eaten boiled with rice
납작보리	napchak pori	crushed barley, parched barley	is called *pori ch'a*, barley tea
비지	piji	bean curd lees	used in soup instead of meat
수수	susu	sorghum, broomcorn, kaoliang	two kinds: *mesusu*, ordinary, and *ch'asusu*, glutinous
쌀	ssal	rice (grain)	two kinds: *mepssal*, ordinary, and *ch'apssal*, glutinous
옥수수	oksusu	maize, Indian corn	eaten on the cob
완두	wandu	green pea	picked fully ripe and boiled with rice
조	cho	millet	two kinds: *mejo*, ordinary, and *ch'ajo*, glutinous
찹쌀	ch'apssal	glutinous rice	for *ttŏk* and festal food
청포	ch'ŏngp'o	mung bean curd	
콩	k'ong	soy bean	*kŏmjŏng k'ong* (black); *hŭin k'ong*. white
팥	p'at	sweet bean	black, white and red varieties
피	p'i	barnyard millet	
햅쌀	haepssal	new season's rice	newly-harvested rice, specially good
현미	hyŏnmi	unpolished rice	
호밀	homil	rye	

MEAT AND EGGS

Korean	Romanization	English	Description
간	kan	liver	of beef, pork, chicken, etc

갈 비	kalbi	ribs	of beef or pork (both highly esteemed)
계 란	kyeran	hen's eggs	*kyeran hŭinja*, white of egg *kyeran norinja*, yolk of egg
기 름	kirŭm	fat (of meat)	this is the general word for oil or fat
닭 (고기)	tak(kogi)	chicken, fowl	
돼 지 고 기	twaejigogi	pork	
쇠 고 기	soegogi	beef	sometimes called *sogogi*
양 고 기	yanggogi	lamb, mutton or goat	lamb is very occasionally available in the shops that cater for foreigners but it is not used in traditional Korean cookery, and most Koreans find it distasteful
천 엽	ch'ŏnyŏp	tripe	
콩 팥	k'ongp'at	kidney	

CONDIMENTS AND SPICES

간 장	kanjang	soy sauce	may be made at home, see Korean recipe-books; a lengthy process. The amounts used in the recipes are right for Korean soy sauce; Chinese and Japanese soy sauce are different, especially in their degree of saltness
깨 소 금	kkaesogŭm	sesame salt	parched sesame seed pounded with salt (see page 14)
계 피 가 루	kyep'i karu	powdered cinnamon	
고 추 고 추 가 루	koch'u koch'u karu	red pepper (chilli) red pepper powder	whole and in the forms listed; the best quality is made by removing the seeds while drying, before grinding
고 추 장 실 고 추	koch'ujang shilgoch'u	red pepper paste red pepper threads	for decoration and mild flavouring

꿀	kkul	honey	traditional sweetener
된장	toenjang	soy-bean paste	for soup
낙화생기름	nak'wasaeng kirŭm	peanut oil	used for frying
미원 아이미	miwŏn aimi	MSG, ajinomoto	much used by some cooks but not, of course, traditional. They are trade names.
생강, 세앙	saenggang, saeang	ginger	the fresh root is available all year, and is used finely chopped or sliced
설탕	sŏlt'ang	sugar	white, lump, light and dark brown are available
소금	sogŭm	salt:	
호렴	horyŏm	rough salt	
고운소금	koun sogŭm	fine salt	
식염	sigyŏm	table salt	
식초	shikch'o	vinegar	this used to need diluting, 1 T to 1 cup water, but diluted vinegar of the strength we are used to is now in the supermarkets; check your vinegar before using it.
청종	chŏngjong	rice wine, 'sake'	a Japanese brand name, commonly used for all clear rice-wine
참깨	ch'amkkae	sesame seeds	from the field sesame
참기름	ch'amgirŭm	sesame oil	from the field sesame; oil from the wild sesame (perilla frutescens) is used for frying, but the strong-flavoured oil used as a spice is *ch'amgirŭm*
청주	ch'ŏngju	correct name for chŏngjong	
초	ch'o	see shikch'o	
후추 (호초)	huch'u (hoch'o)	black pepper	

Index